EDWARD LEAR
AND MY FATHER

EDWARD LEAR AND MY FATHER

LIMERICKS REVISITED

COMPILED BY:

BARBARA WHITEHEAD

authorHOUSE®

AuthorHouse™ UK Ltd.
1663 Liberty Drive
Bloomington, IN 47403 USA
www.authorhouse.co.uk
Phone: 0800.197.4150

Published by AuthorHouse   04/24/2014

ISBN: 978-1-4969-7819-6 (sc)
ISBN: 978-1-4969-7820-2 (e)

FOREWORD

This is really my father's book. Dad was a great fan of Edward Lear, constantly reciting the Nonsense Poems throughout my childhood.

He asked me, when I was a teenager, to quote the first line of a Lear limerick. Without reading the rest of the verse, Dad composed his own version using Lear's first line and he continued until he had rewritten all hundred and nine limericks, bringing them into the twentieth century.

If this little book amuses and delights even a few people, I think Dad would be pleased. His motto in life was to put more into this world than he took out of it. I have tried, out of love for him, to enable him to leave a little more in this world.

Barbara Whitehead (nee Lowe)

There was an old man with a beard
Who said: "It is certainly weird,
But the time that I save,
By neglecting to shave,
Just seems to have all disappeared."

There was young lady of Ryde
Whose mouth was excessively wide.
When she started to smile
It increased by a mile
So she never could do it inside.

There was an old man with a nose
Which was longer than you would suppose.
It reached just half way
From Peking to Bombay,
By the long way—not as the fly crows.

There was an old man on a hill
Who gave the spectators a thrill
By standing alone
On the very top stone
And waving his arms like a mill.

There was a young lady whose bonnet
Had wondrous adornments upon it.
The young men in a daze
Would write verse in its praise
And one even managed a sonnet.

There was young person of Smyrna
Who sat on a lit Bunsen burner.
He got such a fright
When it set him alight,
But you see, he was only a learner.

There was an old person of Chili
Who rode about town on a filly.
He just used to revel
In parts that were level
But hated the bits that were hilly.

There was an old man with a gong
Who beat it when matters went wrong.
The effect that this had
Was to make people glad
And the hearers all burst into song.

There was an old lady of Chertsey
Who refused absolutely to curtsey,
But when they said: "Why?"
Her astounding reply
Was that each time she did it, it hurt, see?

There was an old man in a tree
Who said: "It is dreadful for me—
Because of an adder
Ensconced on my ladder
I cannot get down for my tea."

There was an old man with a flute
Who played in a bullet-proof suit.
For he knew that one day
Someone surely would say:
"I can bear it no longer" and shoot.

There was a young lady whose chin
Was a matter of interest in
The place where she dwelt.
The inhabitants felt
It was quite the wrong shape, and too thin.

There was an old man of Kilkenny
Who once bought a pup for a penny
And it grew, he would boast,
To be equal to most
And very much better than many.

There was an old person of Ischia
Who said: "It is certainly riskier
To serve homemade brew
In the place of a stew,
But it makes all the customers friskier."

There was an old man in a boat
Who cruised in the old castle moat.
Though restricted in scope,
There was rather more hope
If the vessel, perchance, did not float.

There was a young lady of Portugal
Who said to her sister: "I've caught you girl,
Out here in the street
Without shoes on your feet.
Why don't you do what I've taught you, girl?"

There was an old man of Moldavia
Who said: "There is nothing can save yer.
I'll go to a shop
For a razor and strop
And be back in a minute to shave yer."

There was an old man of Madras
Who really was rather an ass
To take a large light
In the dead of the night
Just to look for a leak in the gas.

There was an old person of Leeds
Who sowed all his garden with seeds,
But just like me and you,
All the plants that he grew
Were fifty-two species of weeds.

There was an old person of Hurst
Who laughed till he jolly well burst.
His nephews and nieces
Said sticking the pieces
Together again was the worst.

There was a young person of Crete
Who hadn't a shoe to her feet.
Most people just stared
To see her feet bared
But some thought she looked rather sweet.

There was an old man of the Isles
Who placed all his money in piles.
The sight of his treasure
Produced so much pleasure,
His face was all covered in smiles.

There was an old person of Buda
Whose manners grew every day ruder
But the cook (did she not?)
Took a very large pot
And just popped her in and then stewed her.

There was an old man of Columbia
Who went not to a pub to drink some beer
But stayed in his bed
Eating crackers instead
And the bed became crumby and crumbier.

There was a young lady of Dorking
Whose hobby was painting and chalking
And one could somehow sense
That her work was immense.
Even urchins declared it was corking.

There was an old man who supposed
That a garden grew better when hosed.
He did this each day
Till he washed it away
And left all the foundations exposed.

There was an old man of the West
Who lived like a bird in a nest,
But he said to his wife
That, for comfort in life,
He would say that a house was the best.

There was an old man of the Wrekin
Whose shoes had a musical squeak in
They would play Auld Lang Syne
When the weather was fine
But it rained and they sprang a great leak in.

There was a young lady whose eyes
Were as large as a couple of pies.
Why, even her Ma
(And you know what they are)
Would admit they were rather outsize.

There was a young lady of Norway
Who said: "I am coming round your way
To try to obtain
Some employment for gain.
My finances are in such a poor way."

There was an old man of Vienna
Who married a Spanish duenna.
He complained that her hair
Was uncommonly fair
And compelled her to dye it with henna.

There was an old person whose habits
Made him go for a lettuce and grab its
Most tenderest part
(which is known as the heart)
Just to feed to his numerous rabbits.

There was an old person of Dover
Who tried to subsist upon clover.
He didn't grow fat
While he feasted on that
And was glad when the trial was over.

There was an old man of Marseilles
Who fitted his yacht with new sails.
The vessel just flew
When a gentle wind blew
But it went all to pieces in gales.

There was a old person of Cadiz
Who lived by himself and who made his
Own meals, for he said
He would rather be dead
Than be waited upon by the ladies.

There was an old person of Basing
Who found that his trousers were blazing.
He said: "that is why
The folk who pass by
All stand with their mouths open, gazing.

There was an old man of Quebec
Who went to night school at the tech.
It confirmed his worst fears
As it bored him to tears
And gave him a pain in the neck.

There was an old person of Philae
Who said to his friends, rather shyly:
"Just watch me jump down
From the walls of the town."
But he rated his prowess too highly.

There was a young lady of Bute
Whose hat was decidedly cute.
All over the top
Grew a flourishing crop
Of blackcurrants and similar fruit.

There was a young lady whose nose
Was as useful as most, I suppose,
But it wasn't the kind
You would have in your mind
When awarding the prizes at shows.

There was an old man of Apulia
Who said to his daughter: "Now Julia,
This tap, though marked "hot",
Is most certainly not.
The notice is put there to fool yer."

There was an old man with a poker
Whose wife was a terrible croaker.
He tapped her, in play,
With his poker one day
But he hit her too hard and he broke her.

There was an old person of Prague
Who suffered from palsy and ague,
But the doctors just said
Take it easy—in bed
Which was all most delightfully vague.

There was an old man of the North
Who lived on the banks of the Forth.
Though awkward at times,
This was useful for rhymes
Such as this one, for what it is worth.

There was an old person of Mold
Who suffered severely from cold.
In the Summer he wore
Thirteen waistcoats, or more,
And shivered (or so I've been told).

There was an old man of Nepal
Who stabled his horse in the hall
And his visitors' eyes
Showed dismay and surprise
Whenever they happened to call.

There was an old man of th'Abruzzi
Who pronounced it (quite wrongly) like pussy.
When I pointed this out
He said: "Yes, I've no doubt,
But you see, I am not very fussy."

There was an old person of Rhodes
Who carried enormous great loads.
He said:" I should laugh
If this one comes in half,
But not if it goes and explodes."

There was an old man of Peru
Who got mixed with the apes at the Zoo.
It took, so they say,
The best part of a day
For the keepers to find who was who.

There was an old man of Melrose
Who wore the most ill fitting clothes.
His jacket and vest
Barely covered his chest,
But his shirt was right down to his toes.

There was a young lady of Lucca
Who broke when a bull tossed and shook her.
But some people behind,
With great presence of mind,
Obtained some adhesive and stuck her.

There was an old man of Bohemia
Whose conduct grew dreamy and dreamier.
His relatives thought
That he must have been caught
By a maiden, or else had anaemia.

There was an old man of Vesuvius

Whose language was airy and dubious.

He would not be so plain

As to mention the rain;

It must always be Jupiter Pluvius.

There was an old man of Cape Horn
Who began life the day he was born,
But he drew his last breath
On the day of his death
At about half past six in the morn.

There was an old lady whose folly
Had caused her to tear up her brolly
And so, when it rained,
She got wet and complained
While the others kept dry and were jolly.

There was an old man of Corfu
Who climbed Everest for the view.
Then it started to rain
So he climbed down again
Which I think was a pity, don't you?

There was an old man of the South
Whose manners were rather uncouth.
He would take hunks of bread,
Quite as large as his head,
And stuff two at once in his mouth.

There was an old man of the Nile

Whose temper was perfectly vile,

Nor would the best joke

In the whole world provoke

Him to melt for a second and smile.

There was an old person of Rheims
Who contracted the habit, it seems,
Of retiring to bed
With a hat on his head,
But he had most peculiar dreams.

There was an old person of Cromer
Who sat on the stairs and read Homer.
Though it bored him to tears
He continued for years
And lulled himself into a coma.

There was an old person of Troy
Who foreswore to read news when a boy.
No startling disclosure
Disturbed his composure;
No crisis diminished his joy.

There was an old man of the Dee
Whose sorrows were great as could be.
No one who came near him
Was able to cheer him
So they pushed him at last in the sea.

There was an old man of Dundee
Who suffered from insanity.
Having been for his dole,
He would spend it on coal
Which he threw in small lumps out to sea.

There was an old person of Tring
Who held up his trousers with string.
He always made faces
At those who used braces
Which was an unmannerly thing.

There was an old man on some rocks
Who had a succession of shocks,
For the tide washed away,
In the course of one day,
His pyjamas, his vest and his socks.

There was an old man of Coblenz

Who sang as he sat on a fence,

But before vey long

He abandoned his song

As the pain from the spikes was intense.

There was an old man of Calcutta

Who had an intractable stutter.

When he started to speak,

It took nearly a week

For each word that he wanted to utter.

There was an old man in a pew
Who dreamed he was broken in two.
You may guess his surprise
When he opened his eyes
And he found it was perfectly true.

There was an old man who said: "How
Shall I milk this irascible cow?
Each swish of her tail
Capsizes the pail—
That's the twenty first time up to now."

There was a young lady of Hull
Whose life was exceedingly dull
Till one day in the train,
Having noticed the chain,
She decided to have a good pull.

There was an old man of Whitehaven

Whose beard was as black as a raven

But the folk used to scoff

So he cut bit all off

And he looked so much nicer clean-shaven.

There was an old man of Leghorn
Who went off to sleep in the corn.
Not observing the reaper
Approaching, the sleeper
Had most of his clothing off-torn.

There was an old man of the Hague
Who hated his town like the plague
He said: "Some day perhaps,
I shall pack up my traps
And set out on my cycle for Prague."

There was an old man of Jamaica
Who said to his wife: "Find a baker!"
But he did it, he said,
Not to get any bread
But to find out how long it would take her.

There was an old person of Dutton
Who dined upon pork, beef and mutton.
When they said: "'tis too much",
He just answered that such
Was his habit - but he was a glutton.

There was a young lady of Tyre
Who put her best clothes on the fire
And yelled with delight
On beholding the sight
Of the flames leaping higher and higher.

There was an old man who said: "Hush!
I can see a remarkable thrush.
If you leave me to it
I'll try to lasso it,
But don't crowd around and don't push."

There was an old man of the East
Who tried to make bread without yeast.
He was full of surprise
When the dough didn't rise
But it taught him a lesson, at least.

There was an old man of Kamchatka
Who purchased a shallow and flat car
But he said that he found
It too close to the ground
And he wanted a tall, wide and fat car.

There was an old man of the coast
Whose figure was fatter than most,
But diving and swimming
Produced such a slimming;
He wore himself out to a ghost.

There was an old person of Bangor
Who suffered from boredom and languor
Which all cures that they tried
Only intensified,
So at last they decided to hang her.

There was an old man with a beard
Whose antics were much to be feared.
He had a large boat
Which he shared with a goat
And he rowed while the animal steered.

There was an old man of the West
Who slept with his feet on his chest.
That caused him much trouble
By bending him double
But he said it suited him best.

There was an old person of Annerley
Who said to his offspring: "Now Stanely
Although you're but six,
Your career we must fix
As I think it essential to plan early."

There was young lady of Troy
Who made a remarkable toy
But nobody knew
What the thing ought to do,
So she gave it away to a boy.

There was an old man of Berlin
Who grew most appallingly thin.
'Twas a pity, I think,
That his bones didn't shrink;
They became far too big for his skin.

There was an old person of Spain

Who sowed all his garden with grain.

The birds thought it fun,

But he took a large gun

And thousands and thousands were slain.

There was a young lady of Russia
Who, fearing that people would crush her,
Said: "I'll stay where I am
At the door of the tram."
But they brought a policeman to push her.

There was an old man who said: "Well!
I have married a witch in the dell."
When they said : "How absurd!"
He replied not a word,
But he put them all under a spell.

There was a young lady of Wales
Who carefully painted her nails.
She looked, so they say,
Like an old bird of prey,
But she thought it attracted the males.

There was an old person of Cheadle

Who said : "Now, a jolly good feed'll

Improve me so much

That I'll start learning Dutch

For my mind is as sharp as a needle."

There was a young lady of Welling

Who had an old chest in her dwelling

And stories were told

About pirates and gold,

But I think they improved in the telling.

There was an old person of Tartary
Who used string instead of a garter. He
Must have tied it too tight
When he did it one night,
As he stopped the blood flow in an artery.

There was an old person of Chester
Whose neighbours came round to request her
To lend them a quid,
Which she finally did
Though the incident rather distressed her.

There was an old man with an owl
Whose face wore a lowering scowl
When people referred
To his wonderful bird
As some kind or other of fowl.

There was an old person of Gretna
Who said to each person he met: "Na
Just hurry up mon,
There's a storm coming on
And I'm thinking you're going to get wet na."

There was a young lady of Sweden
Who desired very little to feed on.
    That her slim silhouette
    Gave no cause for regret
Was a matter observers agreed on.

There as a young girl of Majorca
Who was a continuous talker.
The people around
Grew bored with the sound
And decided to bottle and cork her.

There was an old man of the Cape

Whose face was a sour as a grape.

He wanted a monkey

To act as his flunkey

But had to make do with an ape.

There was an old lady of Prague
Who hated her work like the plague.
If this statement applied
To all that she tried
Is uncertain—the records are vague.

There was an old person of Sparta
Who feasted on cheese and tomato.
So wise did he grow
That the king got to know
And made him a knight of the garter.

There was an old man at the casement
Whose spectacles needed replacement.
He leaned out too far,
While observing a star,
And landed somewhere in the basement.

There was a young lady of Clare
Who walked with her head in the air
And she looked very sweet
Till she planted her feet
On a pavement that just wasn't there.

There was an old person of Ems
Who had a collection of gems.
He distributed pearls
To the poor little girls
Whom he met on the banks of the Thames.

There was an old man on whose nose
His wife used to hang out the clothes.
Though it tickled a bit
When the pegs didn't fit,
He got used to it soon, I suppose.

There was a young lady of Parma

Who said that no poison could harm her

So, to make good her boast,

She ate strychnine on toast

And she died, and they had to embalm her.

There was an old person of Burton
Who put his best trousers and shirt on
But he slipped and he fell
And, I'm sorry to tell,
They collected a good deal of dirt on.

There was an old man of Aosta
Who went for a trip down to Gloucester.
It changed his whole life
Since he went with his wife,
And by some misfortune, he lost her.

There was an old person of Ewell
Who suffered from cold something cruel.
Neither coal, coke nor peat
Gave him enough heat
So he cut up his chairs to make fuel.

ABOUT THE AUTHOR

William Joseph Lowe (1910-1975) was born and educated in Liverpool.

He graduated with First Class Honours in chemistry and soon became the chief chemist at William Crawford and Sons, biscuit manufacturers, continuing in this post when Crawford's joined United Biscuits.

A devout Catholic, a keen gardener, an accomplished linguist, "Bill" had many interests and his encyclopaedic knowledge enlightened many.

He loved poetry and always marked special family occasions with his own poetic offering.

He was devoted to his wife, Win, to whom he was married for forty-one years. He was a loving father to Barbara and Bernard and a doting granddad for all too short a time to John, Stephen and Claire.

Lightning Source UK Ltd.
Milton Keynes UK
UKOW03f0506130514

231574UK00001B/9/P